AF594100

A GENTLE WAR

BLOOD AND FIRE
THE SALVATION ARMY
"WHILE WOMEN WEEP, AS THEY DO NOW,
I'LL FIGHT;
WHILE MEN GO TO PRISON, IN AND OUT,
IN AND OUT, AS THEY DO NOW,
I'LL FIGHT;
WHILE THERE IS A DRUNKARD LEFT,
WHILE THERE IS A POOR LOST GIRL

A GENTLE WAR

The Story of The Salvation Army

By Lawrence Fellows/Photographs by Janet Beller

MACMILLAN PUBLISHING CO., INC., New York
COLLIER MACMILLAN PUBLISHERS, London

Illustration facing title page: The Salvation Army Centennial Memorial Temple, New York City

Macmillan Publishing Co., Inc.
866 Third Avenue, New York, N.Y. 10022
Collier Macmillan Canada, Ltd.

Printed in the United States of America

10 9 8 7 6 5 4 3 2 1

LIBRARY OF CONGRESS CATALOGING IN PUBLICATION DATA

Fellows, Lawrence.
A gentle war.

Bibliography: p.
Includes index.

SUMMARY: Examines the history, goals, and work of the Salvation Army.

1. Salvation Army—History—Juvenile literature.
[1. Salvation Army—History] I. Beller, Janet.
II. Title.

BX9715.F44 267'.15 79-14622 ISBN 0-02-734430-4

For Anita
—L. F.

For David Plowden,
who changed the course of my life
—J. B.

Many people helped us with this book, and we want to express our gratitude to all of them, starting with David Reuther, whose idea it was and who did much of the early editing of it. For many years, he had harbored warm feelings and a fair measure of curiosity about The Salvation Army, and assumed that other people besides himself, young and old, would like to know more about this unique institution.

For some insights into The Salvation Army's varied experiences abroad, we are indebted to Lisa and Hannes Becker of Cologne, who helped us trace The Salvation Army's special problems in Germany; and to Stanley Arthur, who was, when the book was being written, British High Commissioner in Fiji.

Many others in the United States and abroad helped in this collaborative effort. The names and faces of some of them appear in this book. They shared with us valuable fragments of their years of ministering to the weary, hungry and troubled people who are the abiding concern of Salvationists everywhere.

For the expert advice and criticism we asked of them, we owe thanks to Frances Weiss and Major Dorothy E. Breen and the others in The Salvation Army's administration who bore with us patiently, and who understood that we had set out neither to praise The Salvation Army nor to scorn it, but only to see it, through its many fascinating parts, in another perspective.

Lawrence Fellows and Janet Beller

In winter a chill wind whistles through derelict buildings and over chunks of broken asphalt in the streets of East Harlem, New York City. Blowing dust and discarded newspapers before it, the wind whips past the stumbling, sometimes motionless, figures of drunks and junkies, prostitutes, beggars, thieves, and other lost souls who drift from shadow to shadow, or lean against the walls for support, or crowd into doorways for shelter. Some of them, in their blurry ecstasy, seem not to notice their discomfort. Some seem to be swept along helplessly by the wind.

On Sundays there is an element of hope. In the evening at the Salvation Army's Manhattan Citadel on East 125th Street, Brigadier Mary Nisiewicz watches the clock on the wall. When it shows 6:30 she strides, confident and full of courage, out onto the battlefield at the head of her tiny brigade—a resolute army of twenty uniformed Christian

Brigadier Mary Nisiewicz in East Harlem

soldiers fighting a gentle war. Among them are old and young, black and white, men in red-banded visor caps and women in midnight-blue bonnets. The sturdy, white-haired brigadier has been going on such forays for forty years. Her troops carry cornets and trombones, alto and baritone horns and tubas, and a big bass drum. Out across 125th Street and over to Lexington Avenue they advance into battle, to preach and pray in the open air, and to play rousing hymns to show people the way out of despair:

Take the name of Jesus ever,
    As a shield from every snare;
If temptations round you gather,
    Breathe that holy name in prayer.

The Manhattan Citadel is but one of thousands of outposts for an army of more than two million men and women fighting for the redemption of people around the world. Out in the front ranks are seventeen thousand Salvation Army officers, nearly four thousand of them in the United States. They have been through the two-year course at one of the Salvation Army's officer-training schools, through prescribed courses of postgraduate study afterward, and then up the ladder of authority: lieutenant, captain, major, lieutenant-colonel, colonel, commissioner. At the top is the general, who is the international head of The Salvation Army.

All officers are ordained ministers of the Gospel. They spread the word of God, and carry comfort wherever they can, in 109 languages in 82 countries, some of them remote

Salvation Army cadets at a service of retirement

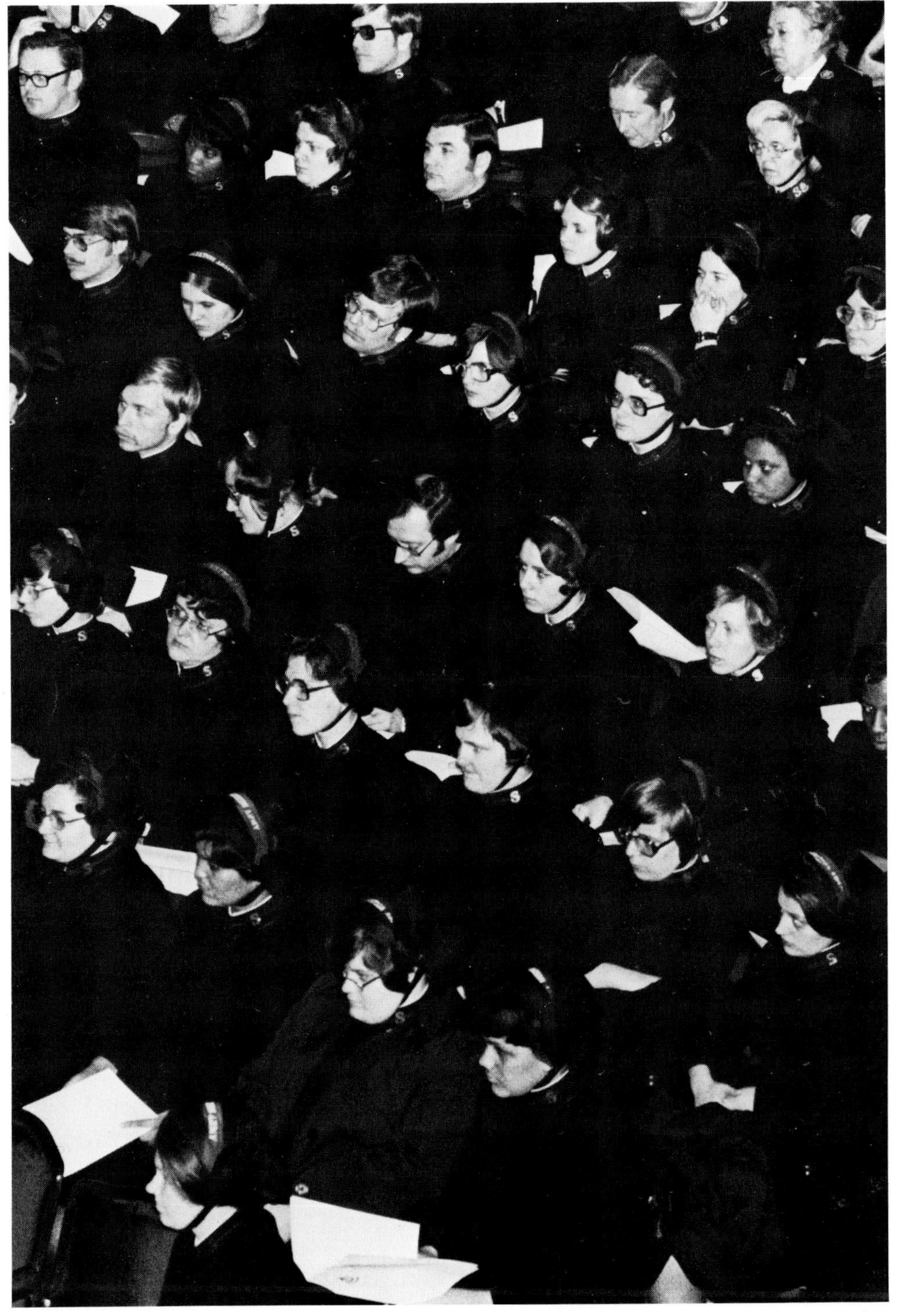

and, at times, hostile. The officers are cared for, too, by The Salvation Army, as long as they serve it faithfully—provided with living quarters and furnishings, and a car, if one is needed; with a modest salary and a pension when they retire. In the end, Salvationists do not die; they are "promoted to Glory."

There are also more than eighty thousand soldiers in this tranquil, tolerant army in the United States alone. Most are men and women who have other jobs, and serve in The Salvation Army part-time. Soldiers wear uniforms when they are on Salvation Army duty, whether playing in the bands at open-air meetings, or teaching the Bible, or assisting officers in their visits to the poor or ailing.

And then there are the two million people in the world, including 366,000 in the United States, who consider The Salvation Army, with its simple Christian services, their church, and work for it when they can.

Among many services, The Army provides neighborhood centers, homes and hospitals for unmarried mothers, a missing-persons bureau, marriage guidance clinics, family welfare agencies, day nurseries, clubs for boys and girls, summer camps for children and for older persons. The Army helps people plan for their old age. It provides disaster relief, offers comfort and counseling for prisoners and parolees, administers residential rehabilitation centers for adults with problems, including alcoholism, and gives a helping hand to drug addicts like those in the streets of East Harlem.

Sometimes as many as eighty addicts a week reel and

A young Army musician at Star Lake Music Camp in New Jersey

stagger into the Salvation Army's Corps Outreach Program next door to the Citadel. Some of them are really desperate characters, like the one known as One-Eye Dutch. He lost his other eye in a fight.

"We encountered him out on the street, really strung out, as they say, I mean, really caught up in drugs," said Joseph Gagos, who started the Outreach Program in East Harlem. "We spoke to him and we impressed upon him that there was a possibility for change, if only he'd respond. And we left it at that," Mr. Gagos said. "About two weeks later he came by the office and said, 'Okay, I'm here. I want to do something about my life. Where do I start?' "

Salvationists worked with him, helped him to believe a bit in himself, eventually arranged for him to enter a drug rehabilitation program in York, Pennsylvania. When he came out of it, he was a new person. He married and settled down, and took a job as a counselor in the program.

Daisy Rivera was so heavily into drugs that she had blacked out once while she was standing at an open window, and fell four stories to a railing. She spent ninety days in a coma, and was still limping when she went to The Salvation Army to ask if there was something that could be done, not for her, but for her husband, who seemed to her to have resigned himself to the sub-culture of the streets and prisons. The Army talked her into first taking care of herself, and found a place for her in a program administered by the Quakers in New York. Eventually she got back on her feet.

"Her husband came out of prison and he saw the spectacular change in her life," Mr. Gagos said. "And he came to us and said, 'Whatever it is that you did for her, I'd like you to do for me.' So we got him straightened out. They bought their own home in the Bronx and they've done well ever since."

Joseph Gagos is not, strictly speaking, an officer or a soldier of The Salvation Army. He was hired by The Salvation Army to work for it, because of the need The Army felt for his special talents. There are nearly twenty thousand Salvation Army employees like Mr. Gagos in the United States, including counselors and specialists of various kinds. They are no less dedicated to The Army because of their different status.

When The Salvation Army called Joseph Gagos and asked him to set up the Outreach Program in East Harlem, he responded right away, starting his program in an old restaurant on East 121st Street until there was room next to the Citadel. He knew what had to be done, and how urgently, for he had been an addict years before, and was pulled back from the abyss in a program administered by the Damascus Church in New York.

"And right after I found the answers for my life," Mr. Gagos said, "I decided that what I wanted to do was reach out and help others."

At Lexington Avenue, close to the Manhattan Citadel, a Salvation Army band stood in a half circle in front of a shuttered army-surplus store. A tambourine, to hold donations, had been put on a frail wooden stand in front of the band.

A tall, lean man who wore platform shoes, a stylish tan cap pulled rakishly down over one side of his face, and dark

Overleaf: An open-air meeting in New York City

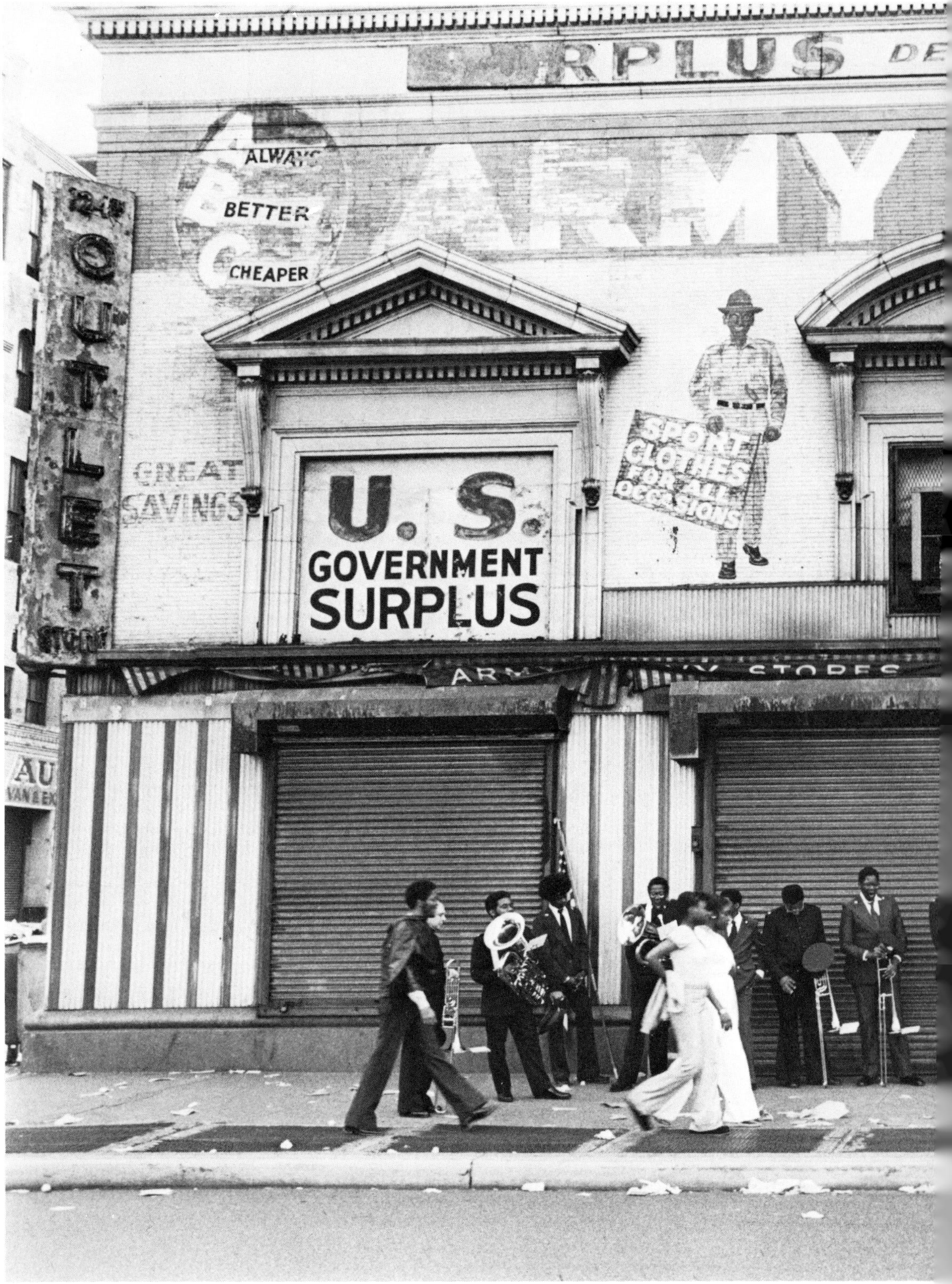

RPLUS DE
ALWAYS
BETTER
CHEAPER
ARMY
OUTLET
GREAT SAVINGS
U.S.
GOVERNMENT
SURPLUS
SPORT CLOTHES FOR ALL OCCASIONS
STORES

ARTMENT STORES
NAVY
ALWAYS
BETTER
CHEAPER
WAR
SURPLUS
NEW & USED
A B C ARMY & NAVY STO

eyeglasses, even in the night, stopped in front of the band, as if he were going to conduct it, and then sat unsteadily on the wooden barrier at the edge of a break in the pavement. The bottle he clutched in his hand was open, but still in its brown paper bag.

A drunk in tattered, outsize clothes stumbled blearily past him to the tambourine and emptied his pockets of change, some of it falling into the tambourine, some into the street. He blinked at the pennies rolling away, but seemed unable to retrieve them.

A young woman watched from the doorway of a luncheonette, and the pale neon light showed anguish in her face. After a few moments, she turned and went inside again.

Francisco Ortiz stood for a while beside the band, then took a dollar from his pocket and dropped it into the tambourine. "They help people," he explained. "Maybe I need them one day."

When the Salvationists returned to the Citadel for the evening service, one woman followed. But she never took a seat. She stood at the back, and finally turned and left. No one had asked to be converted that night.

"We don't get discouraged," Brigadier Nisiewicz said. "We've seen too much good done. You know, people who were really impossible. Really, you'd say 'No hope,' and then they came around and really got straightened up."

The brigadier takes in anyone in need: addicts and prostitutes and abandoned children and anyone else who can use temporary shelter or solace. Her guests sleep in spare beds in the Citadel until other places can be found for them.

Even after years of perceiving need and helping, a veteran like Brigadier Nisiewicz can be surprised, as she was one time when she went to the rescue of an unsteady man some muggers were following.

"I noticed this guy coming down the street and he was really drunk," the brigadier recalled. "And I noticed about five junkies, getting ready. So I walked up to him and I said, 'Listen, mister, you're in trouble. Not only are they going to rob you, but they're going to hurt you.' "

He shushed her, but she persisted. Finally the would-be muggers left. The wobbly man straightened up, quite sober, and said to the brigadier in exasperation, "Thanks a lot, lady, I'm a cop."

"That's a tough area," said Major Lawrence J. Beadle, who was visiting the Manhattan Citadel that night from Divisional Headquarters on West 23rd Street. "There are a lot of hookers and drug addicts, and all sorts of people hang around the street corners, you know. But from my point of view it's where The Salvation Army really should be."

The Salvation Army was founded by William Booth in England more than a century ago. One of its early songs included these lines:

> In the streets, in the lanes, aye, anywhere,
> Our cathedral is the open air.

William Booth's wife, Catherine Mumford Booth, a frail

Overleaf: Salvationists at a marathon open-air meeting

E SALVATION A
MERGEN
MOB

MY
73

woman but a fiery evangelist, would not have been pleased to see the mission of The Salvation Army conducted entirely indoors. In 1880 she wrote in a discourse on the training of Salvation Army cadets:

> It is sentimental hypocrisy to sing "Rescue the perishing, care for the dying" in the drawing-room, to the accompaniment of the piano, without ever dreaming of going outside to do it.

William Booth was born in Nottingham, England, on April 10, 1829. When he was thirteen, his father suffered disastrous financial reverses, and William was apprenticed to a pawnbroker. He despised the work.

By the time he was fifteen, Booth had begun to preach to young people in the streets after working hours, trying to arouse a new religious passion in them, proudly leading a rabble of his ragged, rough-looking new friends into the front pews of the Methodist Church when he could. When he was twenty, he left Nottingham for London and worked, again unhappily, in a pawn shop until closing time each day. At night he preached in the streets.

On his twenty-third birthday, he became engaged to Catherine Mumford, and left the pawnbroking business to be a regular preacher for an evangelistic group known as the Methodist New Connection. He and Catherine Mumford were married three years later.

But after nine years in the ministry, the differences between William Booth and the church had become too great to

On Fifth Avenue, New York City, during the Christmas Kettle campaign

THE SALVATION ARMY
Salem

WHILE THERE REMAINS ONE DARK SOUL,
WITHOUT THE LIGHT OF GOD,
I'LL FIGHT--
TO THE VERY END!"
GENERAL WILLIAM BOOTH

ignore. His evangelistic fervor suited his wife, but was too much for some of the more staid members of the church. When Booth was ordered at a meeting to give up his outdoor revival meetings, Mrs. Booth leaned forward from the gallery and called to him, "Never!"

Booth broke with the Methodist New Connection, and for a while held tent services with another evangelist on an old Quaker burying ground in Whitechapel, London. Then, in July 1865, he formed the East London Revival Society, which soon became The Christian Mission. Most of those who attended his meetings were the same unwanted, desperately poor people he would have in his congregations for the rest of his life. The meetings were held wherever Booth could find room—in a tent, an old dance hall, a storage shed, an old saloon. Mission members marched with him, singing and carrying the mission flag, into the shabbiest districts of London, and from there to other cities. After a year there were three hundred members of The Christian Mission. After four years there were three thousand. They began to refer to themselves as the "Hallelujah Army," and to William Booth as their "general."

In 1878 William Booth was looking over the printer's proofs of the annual report of his mission's activities. He studied the title, "The Christian Mission—A Volunteer Army," and then, with sudden inspiration, crossed out the words, "A Volunteer Army," and wrote in their place, "The Salvation Army." He became the first general of The Army, which in time acquired all the accouterments of a military

A soldier from England gives the Salvation Army salute

organization—uniforms, ranks, flags, a book of orders and regulations, and a rigid code of discipline.

General Booth sent his officers and soldiers on campaigns throughout Britain and abroad. Where he could manage it, he followed. All his life he pushed the Army's battle lines outward—to Canada, Australia, France, Switzerland, India, South Africa, Iceland, and elsewhere, until its message of salvation was spread around the world.

In October 1879 Lieutenant Eliza Shirley, who had traveled from England to the United States to join her parents, held the first American meeting of The Salvation Army in Philadelphia. Afterward she begged her superiors in England for reinforcements.

Six months later Commissioner George Scott Railton and seven women officers arrived in New York. They knelt in prayer at the Battery to give thanks, and then held the Army's first open-air meeting in the United States.

In those days Salvationists had to cope with hecklers and rowdies on the streets. They were not to be regarded lightly, to judge from these bits of history recorded in *Outreach,* a Salvation Army handbook written in England by James Northey:

> In Guildford, the Captain's wife was knocked down, kicked until unconscious only a few yards from the police station. Another woman was so badly injured that she died within a week. The Captain at Shoreham, Sussex, died after being hit by a stone.
>
> Hot coals, tar and burning sulphur were thrown

at William Booth's followers in Whitechapel, London; rotten fish and rocks in Folkestone and lime in Wolverhampton.

In 1882 nearly seven hundred Army people were knocked down, kicked or otherwise hurt on the streets of Britain alone. Twenty-three of them were children.

In the United States The Salvation Army suffered some abuse at the start, too, but it quickly gained respect. In 1886 Grover Cleveland, President of the United States, received a delegation of Salvation Army officers, and gave the organization his official and personal endorsement, as has every United States President since.

Despite the barriers that were sometimes thrown in the path of The Salvation Army, and the violence that was sometimes directed at it, General Booth never lost sight of his mission. When Catherine Mumford Booth died in 1890 after a long and painful illness, he published a book, *In Darkest England and the Way Out,* and dedicated it to her. It contained his proposals for social reform and for helping the poor and woebegone, including employment bureaus, vocational training, farm colonies, factories to provide work for the jobless, homes for young women in trouble, legal assistance and banking services for the poor, traveling hospitals, and a missing-persons bureau.

Much of Booth's dream was realized. The scorn and ridicule he endured for so many years gave way eventually to

Overleaf: The start of the Christmas Kettle campaign in New York City

SALVATION ARMY

THE SALVATION ARMY

THE SALVATION

sympathy and support for his cause. King Edward VII encouraged him, and asked that William Booth be at his coronation in 1902. The sturdy old evangelist had become an accepted figure in England and abroad.

Booth did not take his first world tour until he was sixty-two, but before he died he had traveled five million miles and given nearly sixty thousand sermons. He had seen his loyal band of followers grow into a sprawling international army. At his last public meeting, in Albert Hall in London on his eighty-third birthday, he was as dauntless as ever.

"While women weep as they do now, I'll fight; while little children go hungry as they do now, I'll fight; while men go to prison, in and out, in and out, I'll fight; while there yet remains one dark soul without the light of God, I'll fight," he said. "I'll fight to the very end."

William Booth died four months later, on August 20, 1912. More than sixty-five thousand people viewed his body lying in state at Clapton. Wreaths came from King George, Queen Alexandra, Kaiser Wilhelm, and other prominent people. There were messages from heads of church and state around the world.

Seven thousand Salvationists marched in the funeral procession. Hundreds of thousands of people stood along the route. Traffic in the center of London stood still for nearly four hours while tribute was paid to the man who had built an army to rescue the most despairing and needy people in the world, in some of the most unlikely places.

Officers and cadets in a "Parade of Witness," New York City

The women who went to France for The Salvation Army during World War I became famous for their efforts to make life in that depressing war a bit more bearable. They made apple pies and doughnuts for the soldiers in the trenches. They mended uniforms and, when the soldiers were willing, arranged to save their pay or send it home for them.

Men and women of The Salvation Army played hymns and marches for the soldiers, and conducted Christian services for them in Salvation Army huts. The huts were also made available for Jewish services. On at least one occasion, a Salvation Army hut was used by the Loyal Order of Moose to initiate a new member.

There were Salvationists on both sides of the fighting in that war, as in others. The Salvation Army has always remained an international force, despite the strong pull of national sentiment in Europe and the United States. The Salvation Army's war was against human distress, not against some other army. And that kind of fight could not end with the Armistice. It went on afterward, bringing relief to people who had been displaced or made homeless by the war, to refugees who were hungry, and to families that had been wrenched apart. Officers in The Salvation Army were moved from one country to another, as they continue to be today, sometimes every two or three years, depending on the need.

When the Nazis came to power in Germany in 1933, the Salvation Army commander in Germany happened to be an Englishman, Commissioner William H. Howard. When he was informed by the Nazi authorities that the Salvation

A pre-Christmas hospital visit

HELLO

THE
SALVATION
ARMY

Army's Boy Scouts and Girl Guards would be absorbed into Nazi youth organizations, Commissioner Howard simply disbanded both of the Salvation Army's youth groups and sent the children home.

Eventually The Salvation Army in Germany was required to give up its shelters to the Nazi welfare organization, and most of its other work had to be slowed down. Officers who had been Jews and converted to Christianity were forced to wear on their Salvation Army uniforms the Star of David, a yellow badge to show their Jewish origins.

The Salvation Army had many loyal friends on both sides of Germany's borders. As things got worse for Jews in Germany, The Army helped many escape to Switzerland or Sweden—not only its own officers and soldiers, but Jews who had helped The Army or were known to it.

When World War II ended, there was again an enormous job to be done in caring for refugees and returning prisoners and for thousands of children who had been stranded in evacuation camps or orphaned by the war. The Salvation Army transferred officers from many countries to Germany and elsewhere in central Europe to help the war's victims rebuild their lives in the ruins.

But after the war the Soviet Union was establishing its authority in eastern Europe, and one country after another fell to the Communist allies of the Russians. Communists considered The Salvation Army, with its Christian ethic and its international outlook, a threat to their doctrine, and it was abolished wherever Communists took control. Salva-

A Corps Community Center in a small town

tionists and their families were jailed, and sometimes exiled or killed. Still, for years afterward, many of them continued to meet secretly for prayers and companionship, and to remember their comrades who had not fared so well.

Josef Korbel, a young Salvation Army officer in Brno, Czechoslovakia, was preparing to go to South Africa with his wife and three children to do missionary work. Early in the morning of September 22, 1949, he was awakened by Communist police agents and taken to prison. He was never charged and never given a formal trial, but for ten years was shifted around in half a dozen prisons and work camps—for no other reason, apparently, than that he was a Salvation Army officer and a rather successful evangelist. Even in his dank and rat-infested cells, he held prayer meetings and managed to convert some of the inmates to Christianity, including a supposedly incorrigible prisoner he referred to as Miroslav. The experience is described in a book, *In My Enemy's Camp,* which Brigadier Korbel wrote with Frank Allnutt and published in 1976:

> With tears and heartbreaking sobs, Miroslav's heavy-laden heart opened to our merciful God. How he prayed! Never have I heard such a prayer! For a long, very long time Miroslav talked to God. When he finished, I knew a new child was born into the family of God!

In the early 1950s the Mau Mau rebellion spread over Kenya, which was then still under British colonial rule. Afri-

A bandmaster and lay leader in the East Harlem Corps

WAR
SURPLUS
NEW & USED
A B C ARMY & NAVY

cans who had attached themselves to Salvation Army missions and become Christians suffered heavily at the hands of the rebels. Yet some faithful members stood by the missions, even after most had abandoned them. George Vine, a British journalist, recalled coming across a tiny Salvation Army meeting-hut in an area that had been overrun by the Mau Mau during the rebellion. Over the door were the words *Watu wa Mungu* (Men of God). And inside the hut were two old native men, old "soldiers" of the Salvation Army mission, and apparently all that was left of it. They sat huddled in a corner, blankets wrapped around them to protect them against the cold night air, their bows drawn for what they thought would be a last, desperate fight to save The Salvation Army from the Mau Mau intruders. The old men did not know that the Mau Mau had passed them by many hours before, and so they sat there, waiting stoically for the end.

These are human tragedies brought on by human beings. They can be as destructive as natural tragedies, or more so, and often seem to be just as unavoidable. The Salvation Army cares for both kinds—the woes mankind inflicts on itself, and the ones that are the result of nature's erratic course.

On May 11, 1953, the sky darkened suddenly over Waco, Texas, and a tornado tore into the middle of town. The savage, twisting wind cut into the city like a rampaging freight train, pulling buildings apart and creating havoc. In less than a minute the tornado was gone, but it left in its wake one hundred and fourteen dead and five hundred injured, and many would remain buried for hours under heaps of rubble.

The people of Waco had not really expected the devastating wind. There was an Indian belief that a tornado would not strike at a town by the crooked Brazos River; many people had not even bothered to take shelter when the warning was broadcast by radio.

With other students from Baylor University, Phyllis Depp Cook ran into town in the driving rain to help with the rescue work. The Air Force eventually sent in floodlights so the search of the ruins could go on through the night. Hospitals shifted their patients around and called in all the medical help they could get to cope with the disaster.

From the first few minutes after the tornado had struck, however, people had been on the scene, comforting the injured, finding hot food and clothing for the survivors and taking them to makeshift shelters in the armory, the churches, and elsewhere, providing coffee and sandwiches and doughnuts for the rescue workers.

"These people were not in uniform," Mrs. Cook said. "I think I just flat out asked, 'Where's all this help coming from?' and someone said, 'Well, it's The Salvation Army.'

"My roommate, Wanda Nelson, and I introduced ourselves and asked if we could be helpful, and they said yes, and took us off to a room where there were about eight enormous barrels of laundry soap, you know, detergent," Mrs. Cook continued. "People were sitting there, fixing up little personal packages with bars of soap, and detergent, and

Overleaf: Coffee from a mobile canteen during a fire

S 2 ST.
ONE WAY
THE SALVATION ARMY
THE SALVATION ARMY
TER SERVICES
CANTEEN

THE SALVATION ARMY
731

toothbrushes. Our job was to put two cups of detergent in each sack.

"A nice man came by and asked us our names, and where we came from," she recalled. "It was all very casual. We had helped for a couple of hours. We had done a job, but I think they could have done it just as well without us. We thought nothing of it. But in about a month, my roommate and I got certificates through the mail from The Salvation Army, thanking us for the great help we had been. You know, we had done nothing. They had done it all, yet they were the ones who sent out the thank-you notes.

"And they had said nothing to us about religion. There was no proselytizing, nothing," Mrs. Cook said. "We had wanted a job to do, and they gave it to us. I got the distinct feeling that they were ministering to us. They saw that we needed to do something, and they gave us something to do. It was really very beautiful."

Providing comfort and relief where these things are needed most urgently has always been part of the Salvation Army's ministry. Each year, in the United States alone, The Salvation Army is likely to help a half million dazed or distressed people at fires, floods, coal mine disasters, and wherever else the help is needed.

When the Thames River overflowed its banks in London on January 7, 1928, ten people were drowned in basement apartments. Scores were made homeless. Hugh Redwood, a feisty, hard-bitten Fleet Street reporter who had been in The Salvation Army briefly and then had drifted away, was

"League of Mercy" members on a hospital visit

caught up in it again when a young Salvation Army lieutenant asked him to help her carry a sack of heavy clothing for the flood victims. Mr. Redwood was particularly moved by two young women officers who gave up their own quarters so that an elderly couple who had been made homeless could stay together that night.

Afterward he wrote a book, *God in the Slums,* and donated the royalties to The Salvation Army. He helped establish the National Goodwill League, an auxiliary of The Army in England, and became its first president. He also became the religion editor of London's *News Chronicle* and for years wrote a brief sermon in each Saturday paper. At the bottom of each day's editorial column he wrote *bon mots* like these:

> Is your religion your Steering Wheel, or is it only your Spare Wheel?
>
> Life is a Symphony. We lose at least a third of its Beauty by cutting out the Slow Movement.

No one will ever know how many errant men straightened out their lives because of Heinrich Tebbe, the Salvation Army brigadier who became a legend in the prisons around Berlin in the 1920s.

He was known to the prisoners only as Trumpet Henry, for he went from one prison to another, to stand in a corner or a corridor and play sweet and melancholy tunes on his cornet. Prison routines stopped when Trumpet Henry was playing. The wardens let the prisoners gather around this

A soldier at a marathon open-air meeting

THE SALVATION ARMY
THE SALVATION ARMY
TER SERVIC
ANTEEN

smiling, soft-spoken man, sometimes hundreds at a time, while he played for them and told them simple, humorous stories. Some of the stories led to Bible talks, and when Trumpet Henry knelt to pray, many of the prisoners, and often the wardens, would kneel and pray, too.

Trumpet Henry also talked to the prisoners individually, listening to their problems and offering advice. Often he visited their wives or mothers, taking along on each trip a small bouquet of flowers, gathered from the roadside if possible.

He visited Königsberg, Hoheneck, Plötzensee, Görlitz, Brandenburg, and many other prisons, making a hundred visits or more in a year. Sometimes he took along a choir of Salvation Army cadets from Berlin. Once, when the prisoners at Krielow, a maximum-security prison, learned that Trumpet Henry was coming, they covered the prison gate with ribbons and garlands of flowers. When he arrived they were standing there in a group, singing a German hymn:

Brothers, reach out and join hands . . .

Behind prison walls The Salvation Army has always found a deep well of spiritual need. Wherever they can, Salvation Army officers and counselors visit men and women in prison, offering guidance, conducting church services, seeking to add an element of compassion so often missing in those cold, deadening institutions, and so often missing in the lives of the prisoners themselves.

In some places The Army operates halfway houses for

Right: Harmonica music cheers subway riders in New York City.
Overleaf: A band platform at the Army's Star Lake Music Camp.

306
Please
FULL FARE
EACH CHILD
YEARS and OVER

HALLE

LUJAH

prison inmates who are being prepared for release. When they are making that difficult transition from prison to the outside world, many prisoners feel the need for the comfort and moral support they get by living briefly with a small group of prisoners in a supervised home.

In Fiji, the beautiful, tranquil island group in the Pacific, there is a Salvation Army hostel that for years has provided former prisoners the means to get a quiet new start in life. Serious crime is not a problem in Fiji, but there have been problems frequently with Fijians getting drunk and boisterous, and winding up in court the morning after. Often they are sentenced to short terms in jail, followed by short stays in the Salvation Army hostel to prepare them for their return to village life. Few of the men who leave jail by way of the Salvation Army hostel go back to jail again.

They do, however, leave signs behind of their displeasure with supervision, whether in jail or in the hostel; they invariably leave some part of a job undone, whether it is a single plate unwashed or a corner unswept. It is their small protest against regimentation, even the Salvation Army's gentle variety of it. The Fijian who has been to jail, and stayed afterward in the Salvation Army hostel, can hardly wait to get back to the life of his village.

In more complicated societies, like the United States, there is often no such rush to get away from The Salvation Army. Even after they are released on parole, former prisoners can have temporary shelter and work with The Salvation Army. Sometimes it is easier for a prisoner to be re-

Captain Charles Williams at Rikers Island prison, New York

ARMY

THE SALVATION ARMY
THRIFT STORE

leased on parole if he is willing to make his new start with The Salvation Army. Quite often it is easier for a man to find a permanent job if he can tell a suspicious prospective employer not merely that he has come out of prison, but that after coming out of prison he worked for The Salvation Army. And a man with a job is not so likely to wind up in prison again.

Typically, The Salvation Army spends as much time with the prisoners' families as it does with the prisoners—in supportive counseling, taking care of the children of parents who need to work, providing social and recreational programs for the youngsters. In many cases The Salvation Army, by offering children some alternatives to unpleasant things around them, can keep them from stepping onto the same miserable treadmill that carried their fathers or mothers to prison. If the families live in poor neighborhoods, chances are that they know quite well they can turn to The Salvation Army when they are in serious need.

"We get a call, a frantic, desperate call from a family: 'Our kid has been picked up for shoplifting. He's going to be arraigned at Municipal Court on such and such a date,' " said Captain Charles F. Williams, recalling how The Salvation Army so often gets involved in a young person's life.

As director of the Correctional Services Bureau for the Salvation Army's eastern territory in the United States, Captain Williams knows the routine well. He or someone on his staff will talk to the boy in trouble and to his family. The officer then makes a report to the judge, suggesting that the

A Salvation Army thrift store

boy might benefit from being entrusted to The Salvation Army rather than to an institution that could put him with a group of street-wise and troublemaking youngsters, bring out the worst in him, and eventually make him a hardened criminal.

"Then he's released, if the judge wants to do that," Captain Williams added. "Nine times out of ten the judge will send the boy to us—around New York anyway. We make an agreement. He must be involved with us and we see him once or twice a week, or more, depending on the severity of the problem. These children usually have problems. They do poor work in school, and are often abused at home. They are known to the courts, in one way or another, and to the police.

"And our younger people are doing a more violent type of crime," the captain observed. "They are not just runaways and truants. They're ripping people off. They're hurting people because they're lashing out at society."

Yet Captain Williams is convinced that The Salvation Army has a better answer to the problems than stricter judges and bigger reform schools and prisons. He speaks from experience, for he has been a parole officer, a peace officer in a prison, and a prison chaplain. He also has had some encouraging results from his work with youngsters in the New York area. For nine months The Army worked with twenty-five boys in East Orange, New Jersey, and only two had to return to court. In Freeport, Long Island, none of thirty youngsters had to return.

"Not too long ago my wife and I took about fifteen kids down to Disney World," he said. "We had no trouble with them for a whole week. Now these are kids, many of them with serious problems. I call them pre-delinquents. If people hadn't intervened at the appropriate time, they definitely would have landed on the corrections treadmill.

"These kids developed the trip themselves," Captain Williams said. "They raised over two thousand dollars on their own to go on this trip—candy sales, car washes, paper drives, that kind of stuff—you name it, they did it.

"Some officers would definitely disagree with me," he said, "but from where I sit and from what I see coming through the courts, the fact of the matter is we've touched them. Most of the guys know about The Salvation Army."

The Salvation Army is perhaps most famous for the shelter and work it provides for tens of thousands of men whose lives have been shattered by some physical or emotional encounter in the past, and who cannot find the confidence in themselves to rebuild. Many drink, and trust the effects of cheap wine or whiskey to swirl over their minds gradually, like an incoming tide, and sweep their problems out into a vast, meaningless sea.

William Booth, founder of The Salvation Army, set up the first shelters for men like these when he discovered hundreds of them huddled in the cold under the low arches of the London Bridge because they had nowhere else to go.

"Find a building large enough to house these poor wretches," the old general commanded his son and deputy, Bramwell. "Find some way to heat it and get blankets for the men to lie upon."

Today The Salvation Army has 116 Adult Rehabilitation Centers in the United States. More than seventy thousand men, and some women, are housed and fed and given temporary work there each year. They clean and repair furniture, clothes, toys, tools, appliances, books, and other donated articles, and sell them at bargain prices to the public. The real profit, however, is that each one has something useful to do, to help overcome despair.

"It's part of the therapy," said Horace Sellers, a counselor employed at the Adult Rehabilitation Center on Homestead Avenue in Hartford, Connecticut. "Each one has a job to do. We try, as much as possible, to get everyone involved. A person wants much less time to think."

There are usually seventy men in the Hartford center. They may stay a year, or sometimes more, if it seems to help them.

The center provides a library, a music room, playing rooms with card tables and pool tables, a shuffleboard game, and other facilities and programs. On Wednesdays the men meet in a group to talk over problems and progress.

On one Wednesday Mr. Sellers had collected an assortment of advertisements for things like dinette sets and new Cadillacs. "I'm just going to pass this stuff out. We'll talk about what we would do if we wanted them, and what the other fellow would have to do to sell them, and why we don't want them.

"And if we don't want them, what do we want?" he asked. "My thing is I would want more understanding for

At the Adult Rehabilitation Center, Chicago

dip
dots

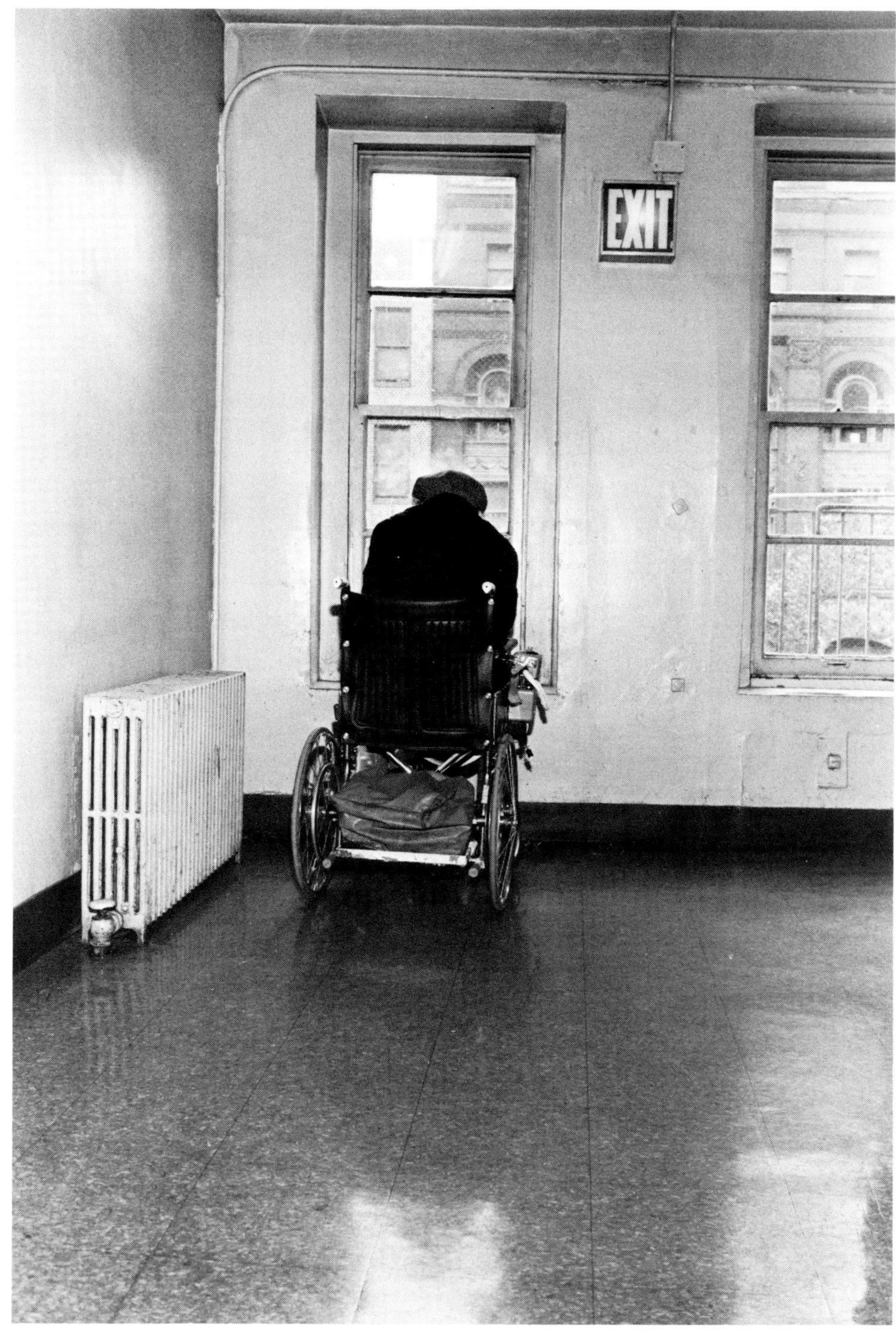
EXIT

each of us of our own priorities. You know, 'What should I do for myself? Who should I go to for help?'

"One time I read something called 'A loser is . . . ,' with little gems like 'A loser is a piano player in a marching band,' " the counselor said. "I just read that and everybody sat around laughing, and we talked about losers, and we talked about winners.

"We all have problems, and as human beings we have to face certain issues together," Mr. Sellers observed. He should know. At one time alcoholism almost had destroyed his life, yet he had made the long, arduous climb back to self-respect, as he is now helping the men in the Hartford center to do.

"I need the therapy, too," Mr. Sellers said, "as much as anyone else."

For most of the tired, disillusioned men on the Bowery, in New York City, there is no hope of climbing back. This is the end of the line.

Not all of the men in Booth House II, the Salvation Army shelter on the Bowery, are alcoholics. Some are mentally disturbed. Some have severe physical handicaps, and have been there for years. Some have spent so many years in prison they can no longer face life outside an institution of some sort. Some, as in Booth House I, which is on Whitechapel Street in London, are merely old and unable to cope alone. There are many such shelters around the world, some for men and some for women, and each seems to have its own special character.

In Booth House II

"Our clients are handicapped people," said Major John Edeen, a Salvation Army officer with broad shoulders, a full Swedish face, and straight blond hair. He has managed Booth House II for eleven years.

"The criterion is a handicap," he said. "And we're not particular what kind of handicap they have."

Booth House II had been a hotel in the days when the Bowery was a place where working men lived, before the street was more or less abandoned to the drunks and derelicts who are drawn there now like pins to a magnet.

About three hundred and eighty men live at Booth House II, but as many as two thousand inexpensive hot meals a day are served to men who come in off the street to eat. Because the old hotel dining room was not big enough, Major Edeen turned the chapel into a cafeteria. Some high-ranking officers in The Salvation Army were a bit startled.

"To them, a chapel is sacred," Major Edeen said. "To me, it was a big room. We had to have a lot of space."

The major also let the men smoke in the cafeteria. He shrugs off smoking as a simple pleasure he would not deny men who have so little else that is pleasurable in their lives.

"I got guys that drink," the major said. "I got guys that smoke. They play cards. I do a lot of tolerating. It works out. If I didn't, I would drive a lot of people away, and that's not what I'm here for."

Major Edeen is not organizing a small mutiny. Fortunately, there are some differences between The Salvation Army and most other armies, apart from the kinds of battles they fight. For one thing, there is no saluting in The Salvation Army. For another, the discipline is a bit less rigid than in some other armies. Although the chain of command leads downward from the general, through his chief of staff, into the different countries, only the broader aspects of policy are normally handed down that way. The priorities and the day-to-day work, for the most part, are left to the people in the "territories" to sort out, and there are four of these in the United States alone, with headquarters in New York City, Chicago, Atlanta, and San Francisco.

There is also a national commander in New York, but his role is really that of coordinator for the four territories. The territorial commanders, who are closest to the problems, are the ones who must decide how to deal with them.

There is one other important difference in The Salvation Army: If an officer does not like it, he can leave it whenever he wants.

In twenty-three years in The Salvation Army, Major Edeen left it only once. After eight months away he went back, convinced that if he fought enough against the directives and discipline he thought were wrong, he could eventually do what he wanted, and do it his way. He has been assigned to eight other places in his career, all in the United States. After eleven years in the Bowery, he feels he will not be moved again, and is doing what he had set out to do.

Although the chapel has been turned into a cafeteria, the billiards room has been made into a bright new chapel, with pale blue walls, chairs of chrome and molded orange plastic, and fluorescent lights fastened to the ceiling. Simple, framed religious slogans hang like pictures on the walls.

Without being pushed to it, the men file in on Sundays, sometimes twenty or thirty of them, to hear Major Edeen preach at the small wooden altar. The flag of the United States stands at one side. At the other is the red Salvation Army flag, with the slogan "Blood and Fire"—blood for the sacrifice Jesus made for human souls; and fire for life, represented by the Holy Spirit.

"Let your mind carry you away," the major said at one Sunday morning service. "Your mind can do wonderful things for you. It can transport you out of this place up to the Waldorf Astoria. Try it. By your faith, God will move into your lives and make it happen."

Then, at a signal from the major, Anna Zenone St. Louis pulled her seat closer to the upright piano at the back of the little room, pulled the collar of her coat tight, and began to play. The men sang:

Trim your feeble lamp, my brother;
Some poor seaman, tempest-tossed,
Trying now to make the harbor,
In the darkness may be lost.

In the Brownsville section of Brooklyn, New York, devastation and the victims of it are everywhere. This was a neighborhood of honest, hard-working people twenty years before. But in the shifting patterns of life in the city, earlier residents of Brownsville left, and behind them, drifters and predators and homeless poor people moved in.

Some tenement owners simply abandoned their buildings when they could not collect the rents they wanted or pay the taxes that were demanded of them. Some landlords

An officer on neighborhood visitation

THE SALVATION ARMY
S
S

set their buildings on fire in order to collect the insurance on them. Thieves found that fires could destroy the traces of a robbery. Pipes and plumbing were stripped from empty buildings and sold as scrap. The streets became unsafe. Police and firemen ventured uneasily into Brownsville while it was falling apart, and now almost nothing remains of vast parts of the neighborhood but the blackened, burned-out shells of buildings.

Almost no one stays in Brownsville but the people who cannot go elsewhere, or dare not. Some of them have slipped into the country illegally from Haiti, the Dominican Republic, Trinidad, or other countries, and cannot follow the others into public housing in other neighborhoods for fear of giving themselves away. So they live in abandoned buildings.

But in the middle of this devastation stands a splendid new brick building, looking somehow like a phoenix with its brilliant plumage rising from the ashes. It is a Salvation Army Corps Community Center run by Captain George Evans, a black man from Harrisburg, Pennsylvania, with a trim beard, a soothing voice, and a will like iron.

"It's a very difficult community. It's the worst in Brooklyn. The buildings look as if they've been bombed out, you know," he said. "People have come in here and said to me on occasion, 'Man, this looks like it went through the Second World War.' "

There had not been a Salvation Army center in Brownsville before; when it was a quiet, settled neighborhood, there probably wasn't as much need for it. But the destruction set in fast, and the need became great. In this case, The Army departed from its customary gradual approach.

"The Salvation Army normally says, 'Now, if you're going to go into a new area, well, let's rent a store front first and see how well you do there,' " Captain Evans said.

"If the people rally behind you, then maybe, after two or three years of being in that store front, they'll move you someplace else," he added. "And then, maybe, after you've proven yourself there and you've outgrown that facility, they'll consider building a building, you know, a new building.

"But they came into this community where there was no program before, absolutely nothing, and they made this commitment, this beautiful facility," the captain said. "And a commitment, you know, is an investment in people."

Before the building was finished, two hundred and fifty youngsters had enrolled in the youth programs: Scouts and Cubs for boys, and Guards and Sunbeams for girls; summer camps and day camp for children during the school vacation months; day care for young children of working mothers; after-school tutoring for pupils who need it; Sunday School.

For church services on Sundays, sometimes seventy-five people come. When the center organized an international dinner and people were invited to bring dishes from their native countries, more than three hundred people came with dishes from a dozen countries in Central and South America, the West Indies, and Africa.

"The Salvation Army has been putting that love we've been talking about into action, that compassion into action in a practical way," the captain said. "They come here and

Overleaf: A playground at the Brownsville Corps Community Center

see we're not done. They look around and can't wait for the gymnasium to get finished; they can't wait for the Senior Citizen Center to open.

"Some of these people have been Baptists over the years. Some of them have been Pentecostal. And, you know, with The Salvation Army coming in new, sometimes they don't want to break their ties with their own religious backgrounds. That's all right, too. The Salvation Army is for all people and we make a policy of that, particularly here," Captain Evans said. "No matter who comes in here, we treat them as people. We don't look at them as black and white, Spanish and Haitian. They're people."

Because The Salvation Army was new to the people of Brownsville, Captain Evans had to establish himself in a uniform that, to his new neighbors, looked strangely out of place on a black person. They seemed to associate The Salvation Army with white persons, and at first they took Captain Evans for a bellhop or a security guard. He also had to establish some tough new rules of neighborhood morality, as he recalled having to do in Pittsburgh, where he had spent three years a decade earlier.

"I overheard some teenagers there one Christmas saying, 'Well, look at that, the white man gets a Christmas tree set up here, nice lights all around, and what did they ever do in our area: nothing,' " Captain Evans remembers them complaining.

"So without saying anything I went to someone and asked about getting a Christmas tree donated, and I got a

Captain George Evans in Brownsville

IRVING TRUST COMP
THE SALVATION ARMY
Sharing is Caring

thirty-foot tree. I went to all the families and collected twenty-five cents from each, for lights and for candy for the kids. Some people said, 'You know, you're crazy for putting that tree up out there. It's going to be stripped in no time.'

"We sent out invitations," the Captain continued. "We were expecting maybe two or three hundred people. Over eleven hundred people showed up for the Christmas-tree-lighting ceremony.

"And sure enough, every light on that tree was gone. The only thing left on the tree was tinsel. And some fellows, you know, came up to me, some of these teenagers who are always trying to be tough—sixteen, seventeen years old: 'Ha, ha, ha, captain, we know who has the lights from the tree.'

"I said, 'I'm not concerned about who has the lights from the tree. But I'll tell you one thing. You guys are the ones who always come up to me and come up to other people and say, "You know, whitey has this and whitey has that and we ain't got nothing."

" 'Whitey didn't come here and take the lights from the tree. You took them.' I said, 'Your families helped to pay for them.' I said, 'Therefore, you were stealing from yourselves, rather than from me. If you think you ripped me off, you're crazy.'

"The very next day, four of the six strands of lights came back," the captain said. "And I heard that all six of them came back finally."

During the Christmas Kettle campaign

He has not forgotten that in a tough neighborhood, candor and firmness pay.

"That's one of the reasons you don't see the writing here you see on all the other buildings," Captain Evans said. "Of course, another thing that helps, too, is that if I catch them writing on the building, I go right outside, give them a steel wool pad. They not only clean their spot, they clean every spot that I can find."

It seemed to Captain Evans that he had known nearly always that he wanted to be a Salvation Army officer. He had been going to Sunday School and social meetings at The Salvation Army from the time he was nine.

"I made a commitment to the Lord that I wanted him to take control of my life, and for whatever purpose he wanted. . . . And going to The Salvation Army, I was confronted about the ministry when I was old enough, and about full-time service in The Salvation Army as an officer. And I felt and I believe this is what the Lord wanted me to do, so I made a commitment. I applied to become an officer in The Salvation Army."

For his wife, Carmen, the association with The Salvation Army had started even earlier. She was only five, on her way home from school one day with an older brother, when a Salvation Army officer stopped them and asked if they would like to attend Sunday School.

"The first thing we said was, 'We can't go unless my mother says we can.' So he came to the house and he explained about The Army and Sunday School, that they tell Bible stories and stuff like that," Carmen said. "And my mother thought it was a good idea, even though it wasn't

Catholic. It was just Christian, and so we all went, even my younger sister. We got so wrapped up in the activities.

"I first felt the Lord wanted me to be an officer when I was about fifteen. It was about the time my mother died, so I pretty much put it in the back of my mind and left it.

"When I was about eighteen I felt it again," Carmen Evans said. "I couldn't resist. It was something that if I couldn't do it, I wasn't going to be happy. I had a job. I was working. I was going to church. But, you see, I just felt as if I should be doing something else. My family felt I should move into the church because I was doing so much there, teaching Sunday School and Sunbeams. Even with that I just didn't feel I was doing enough. I wasn't doing what the Lord actually wanted me to do."

She met George Evans when he was an assistant officer in Hartford for a summer. She was only sixteen at the time. Not until six years later, when she was a cadet in the Salvation Army's School for Officers' Training, did they start seeing each other. They dated for the two years she was a cadet, then married a week after she was commissioned as a lieutenant.

Neither Carmen nor George Evans could have married anyone outside The Salvation Army and remained an officer, even if the other was a soldier, or lay member of The Army. The officer would have to give up his or her commission, although that person could still be a lay member of The Army. The rule is harder on the women in The Salvation Army than it is on the men, because women in The Army usually out-

Overleaf: Young soldiers of The Salvation Army

TO THE GLOR
IN COMMEMORAT
OF THE SALVATIO
VNDER THE DISTIN
ANDER
MEMOR

OF GOD AND
ON OF THE WORK
RMY IN AMERICA

number men by three to one, in the United States at least. The result is that many women officers never marry. But neither George nor Carmen Evans would have wanted the freedom to marry someone outside The Salvation Army.

"There are several reasons for the rule," Captain Evans said. "I think one of the strongest is that The Salvation Army wants to have officers who are dedicated to the ministry and the work of the Lord and The Salvation Army."

Married officers work together in their appointments, and both the wife and husband are expected to share in preaching, teaching, and supervising activities of groups under their command. If the husband dies, the wife is expected to take an appointment.

"In The Salvation Army we both have the same ministry, the same goals and calling," he said.

In The Salvation Army Carmen is called Mrs. Captain Evans, but only because her husband is a captain. She was a lieutenant for the week between the time she was commissioned and her wedding day, when she assumed her husband's rank. Even if she had been a general, she would have become Mrs. Captain Evans.

If her husband dies her title will change from Mrs. Captain Evans to Captain Mrs. Evans, and everyone will know she is a widow. If she had stayed single and become a captain in her own right, she would have been Captain Garay, and everyone would have known she was single.

George is called Captain Evans whether he is married, a widower, or single.

A Salvation Army officer family

Although both are officers and both work, they get one modest paycheck, and it is made out to him.

All of this strikes the women's liberation groups as prejudicial.

"They did picket our Christmas Kettle stands when we were in Newark, but it didn't do any good," Mrs. Captain Evans said. "There's not much they can do about it. It's Army policy.

"It doesn't make any difference to me, anyway," she said. "If you're a good Christian, once you get to heaven they don't have any ranks anyway. All the ranks disappear."

Speaking generally about the equality of men and women Salvation Army officers, Major Dorothy Breen said, "There have been some inequities, but they have been a reflection of the American culture. The Army has come a long way in this area in the past fifteen years."

Major Breen never has married, and has spent most of her twenty-five years as a Salvation Army officer on the staff of the School for Officers' Training, and in territorial headquarters in New York, dealing with publications and research. "I don't think anyone ever said, 'This is a woman. She can't do that,' " Major Breen said. "Women in The Army are given as much work to do as any man, and are expected to do it as well. We're here to work."

"I was a Methodist. I chose The Army because of the great opportunities it offered for service to mankind. The Army financed both my undergraduate and graduate degrees at New York University. Would that have happened if they didn't want a woman to get ahead?

"The Salvation Army said, over a hundred years ago, that women should have equal rights in the church with men. It started with Catherine Booth, wife of the founder."

Mrs. Booth was a slightly built woman, gentle-looking, seeming rather deceptively timid. But in her own quiet, determined way she could enchant an audience, almost like a dealer in magic and spells.

She designed the Army's flag and the famous poke bonnet. But, more than anyone else, she was responsible for the measure of liberation enjoyed by women in The Salvation Army. At first William Booth did not like the idea of women in the pulpit. But the persuasive Mrs. Booth soon changed her husband's mind. More than a century before most other churches began their anguish and uncertainty over the role of women in the ministry, The Salvation Army was accepting women as preachers quite naturally. Mrs. Booth was among them.

She preached that women had no reason to believe they were somehow intellectually or morally inferior to men, certainly not that they were naturally so. She sprang to the defense of women who wanted to preach, and to the attack against Biblical scholars and clergymen who would deny them that right. In 1859 Mrs. Booth wrote a pamphlet, "Female Ministry; or Woman's Right to Preach the Gospel."

"God has given to woman a graceful form and attitude, winning manners, persuasive speech, and, above all, a finely-toned emotional nature, all of which appear to us eminent natural qualifications for public speaking," she wrote.

"Thank God the day is dawning with respect to this

subject,'' Mrs. Booth concluded. ''Women are studying and investigating for themselves. They are claiming to be recognized as responsible beings, answerable to God for their convictions of duty; and, urged by the Divine Spirit, they are overstepping those unscriptural barriers which the Church has so long reared against its performance.''

In her fifty-ninth year, she learned she had cancer and had only two years to live. Her husband, who was preparing to go on an evangelistic mission to the Netherlands, was stunned when he heard the verdict, and assured her he would stay at her side.

''You will do no such thing,'' she insisted. ''Go to Holland and preach. There are people over there who are not ready to die; I am!''

She gave her last sermon from the pulpit of the City Temple in London on June 21, 1888, and then retired to her home in Hadley Wood. For as long as she could, she stayed active in The Salvation Army, mapping plans for it, discussing its problems and its future with her husband and children, among them her daughter Evangeline, who was to become the first woman to lead The Army. On October 4, 1890, Catherine Mumford Booth died in her husband's arms.

Her daughter, Evangeline Cory Booth, became the first woman to serve as general of The Salvation Army. She did much to refashion it, to make it more suited to a modern world. Much of the independence that is permitted the national commands was inspired by her, and many of the busi-

An officer at the Tom Seay Service Center, Chicago

nesslike innovations in the handling of Salvation Army affairs were introduced during her administration.

Yet she had the same fiery, evangelistic spirit as her parents, to judge from the receptions she got in Europe and the United States, and the manner in which people were drawn to her.

In 1896 her father had sent her to New York to persuade some American Salvationists to give up their attempts to break away from the international Army and form a national organization of their own. Evangeline Booth was hissed and booed when she stepped up onto a platform to speak at one meeting. She waved a small American flag and shouted, "Hiss that if you dare!" The stunned crowd fell silent and soon was with her, cheering her appeals to their allegiance.

Two years later, when she was the Salvation Army commander in Canada, Evangeline Booth went to Alaska to arrange for chapels and nursing homes to be built among the gambling halls, saloons, and brothels that had sprung up in the Klondike gold rush. She never got to the Klondike, but accompanied a group of Salvationists as far as Skagway. There she remained to await transportation back to headquarters. Not wanting to waste an opportunity, she preached in the open air in Skagway to twenty-five thousand gold miners, who sat on a mountainside and sang hymns with her.

Afterward she was approached by Soapy Smith, a notorious sinner who had made his name in Denver selling soap on street corners. Inside some of the wrappers were five- and ten-dollar bills, and he did a brisk selling business. People who worked for him were spread through the crowd, pretending to be buyers. Of course, they always got the money-wrapped soap bars.

In Skagway Soapy Smith had developed a reputation as a desperate outlaw, and his own crowd of gunfighters always went with him. Yet he took off his hat when he approached Evangeline Booth.

"I'm Soapy Smith, and I've come to tell you how much I enjoyed your singing," he said.

"Thank you, Mr. Smith," she replied. "Supper is over, but we'd be happy to give you a cup of cocoa."

After cocoa she talked with him for three hours, and then they knelt together. In tears, Soapy Smith promised to mend his ways, to stop killing people and give himself up to the law.

Soon afterward, however, he was ambushed and killed in a gunfight with a committee of citizens of Skagway.

Evangeline Booth became the national commander in the United States in 1904, and stayed there for thirty years. With the help of the United States Army, she sent Salvationists to the front in World War I to serve coffee and pies and doughnuts to the soldiers.

When Armenians were being massacred by Turks, she arranged for survivors to be cared for in Canada. She organized help for India when it was ravaged by famine, and for Japan after it was torn by earthquake. When she was not otherwise overwhelmed with work, she played a prominent role in the women's suffrage movement, helping to win the right to vote for women in the United States. She became a citizen in 1923, three years after that right had been won.

She went to London in 1934 to be elected general of The Salvation Army, and then returned to New York, where a flotilla of harbor boats welcomed her with horns and sirens blowing and streams of water filling the air. She was given a ticker-tape parade through Manhattan, led by the Sixteenth Infantry band, with four Salvation Army bands in the procession.

In 1939 she retired to her country home in Hartsdale, New York, and limited her Salvation Army work to occasional counseling, and to composing Salvation Army songs.

She was a great favorite of American Salvationists, and she had a great love for them in return. She did not accept the criticism that she had set too large an ideal for them, too difficult a task.

"Can *anything* be too hard for Americans or too difficult for America?" she asked.

Evangeline Booth died on July 17, 1950, at the age of eighty-four.

In spite of the obstacles that were thrown in the path of The Salvation Army in its early years, despite the wars and insurrections that broke the Army's ranks in some countries or drove it underground, it has grown to be a formidable international organization.

But the discipline that helped save it also has caused some of its officers and soldiers to leave The Army. One who gave up her rank as an officer but chose to continue as a sol-

The Salvation Army crest at New York territorial headquarters

BLOOD AND FIRE
THE SALVATION ARMY

THE SALVATION ARMY
CENTENNIAL MEMORIAL TEMPLE
WELCOME to
"DISCIPLES OF JESUS"
CADETS SESSION
HERE
SUNDAY SEPT. 19
2:30 P.M. MEETING
5:45 P.M. of WITNESS
7:00 P.M. MEETING

dier was Lieutenant Janet Robinson, who worked with Brigadier Nisiewicz at the Manhattan Citadel in East Harlem.

When Janet Robinson graduated from Ithaca College in New York in 1969, The Salvation Army seemed a convenient way to resolve her uncertainties about a teaching career. But she never grew quite certain of her mission in The Army. From the time she finished her training as a cadet, she never felt comfortable in her uniform. Sometimes, seeking anonymity, she went through the streets of East Harlem in casual clothes.

"In uniform I feel very stared at," Lieutenant Robinson said when she was still an officer. "When I'm in uniform, if I see something happen that I really ought to get involved in, lots of times I think, well, if I get involved and do the wrong thing, then people aren't going to like The Army. And if I'm just a plain old person in blue jeans, then all they can hold it against is a person in blue jeans, you know."

At the open-air meetings, Lieutenant Robinson did not talk much. She gave quiet encouragement to the people who seemed to want encouragement, and handed out copies of *The War Cry*, the Army's illustrated, official weekly publication. *The War Cry* contains reports about Salvationists, stories of human need and the response to it, lists of missing persons who have been reported to The Salvation Army, and accounts of individuals whose lives were changed when they turned to God. Salvationists call the stories in the magazine their spiritual ammunition.

Lieutenant Robinson would like to have spent more of

Before a "Welcome to Cadets" ceremony, New York City

her time talking to individuals, and less of it preaching to the small crowds. She would have preferred music more in keeping with the times, with guitars and amplifiers instead of the brass band. She wanted to feel more certain that she was really leading people to redemption.

"I'm very loyal to The Army in many, many ways," Lieutenant Robinson said. "I've no real gripes as a soldier, only as an officer. It's still the ideal religion to me—it's simple, it's practical. It's not just me thinking about getting my family to heaven. We're trying to help people live well here, as well as getting them to heaven.

"Pretty much, I guess, it's just the way I feel people should live, accepting people where they are," she said. "The Army is more than a do-gooder organization. It tries to go deeper than surface things.

"As far as the Lord calling me and things like that,. I believe that God prepares our whole life for us. Because of the kind of work I've done in The Salvation Army, I've gotten experiences I wouldn't have had. I think the Lord is just preparing me for something else."

On the streets at Christmas, Lieutenant Robinson had stood with fingers so cold and stiff she could hardly play the accordion. She had wished she could perform her mission in her own way, perhaps helping people in need more directly and more swiftly, not just standing there in the cold on New York's Fifth Avenue, waiting for shoppers to drop money in the kettle.

No such doubts troubled Brigadier Mary Nisiewicz, her

Reentering the Centennial Memorial Temple after a "Parade of Witness"

THE SALVATION ARMY

commanding officer at the Manhattan Citadel. While the other Salvationists in the group were playing Christmas tunes, the brigadier was smiling warmly, striding up to people to speak to them and hand them copies of *The War Cry*. She seemed to thrive in the cold and to enjoy each thrilling flush of wind as if it were bringing the promise of spring. And if some shoppers brushed past, her spirit was undaunted.

"Well, I'm not a person who gets discouraged," she said. "If they're interested, they'll smile and stop and talk, whether they have any money or not. If they're really not interested, they'll just keep on going.

"I don't care what it is that you do," the brigadier said. "You're doing it for somebody else. You're not doing it for yourself. That's my philosophy.

"Whatever my duties and responsibilities are, I do them. It's another opportunity to meet people," she said. "So I don't get discouraged, because I feel I'm in it for God."

For Further Reading

BEGBIE, HAROLD. *The Life of General William Booth, the Founder of The Salvation Army*. New York: The Macmillan Company, 1920. (Two Volumes)

BOOTH, BRAMWELL. *Echoes and Memories*. New York: George H. Doran Co., 1925.

BOOTH, EVANGELINE, and HILL, GRACE LIVINGSTONE. *The War Romance of the Salvation Army*. Philadelphia: J. B. Lippincott Company, 1919.

BOOTH, MAUD B. *Beneath Two Flags*. New York: Funk & Wagnalls, 1890.

BOOTH, WILLIAM. *In Darkest England and The Way Out*. New York: Funk & Wagnalls, 1890.

CHESHAM, SALLIE. *Born to Battle: The Salvation Army in America*. New York: Rand McNally & Company, 1965.

COLLIER, RICHARD. *The General Next to God: The Story of William Booth and The Salvation Army*. New York: E. P. Dutton & Co., 1965.

ERVINE, ST. JOHN. *God's Soldier: General William Booth*. New York: The Macmillan Company, 1935. (Two Volumes)

GRUNER, MAX. *Revolutionäres Christentum.* Band II. Berlin: Verlag der Heilsarmee, 1954.

KORBEL, JOSEF; with ALLNUT, FRANK. *In My Enemy's Camp.* Orange, California: Christian Resource Communications, 1976.

NEAL, HARRY EDWARD. *The Hallelujah Army.* Philadelphia: Chilton Co., Book Division, 1961.

NICOL, ALEX M. *General Booth and The Salvation Army.* London: Herbert and Daniel, 1911.

RAILTON, GEORGE SCOTT. *Heathen England.* London: S. W. Partridge, 1877.

REDSTONE, J. J. R. *An Ex-Captain's Experiences of The Salvation Army.* London: Christian Commonwealth Publishing Co., 1888.

REDWOOD, HUGH. *God in the Slums.* New York: Revell, 1931.

REDWOOD, HUGH. *God in the Shadows.* New York: Revell, 1932.

ROOPER, REV. W. H. *General Booth and The Salvation Army.* Bournemouth, England: Bright & Son, 1892.

THOMPSON, PHYLLIS. *The Midnight Patrol.* New York: Hawthorne Books, Inc., W. Clement Stone, Publisher, 1974.

WATSON, BERNARD. *Soldier Saint: George Scott Railton, William Booth's First Lieutenant.* London: Hodder and Stoughton Ltd., 1970.

WISBEY, HERBERT ANDREW. *Soldiers Without Swords: A History of The Salvation Army in the United States.* New York: The Macmillan Company, 1955.

Index